GUIDE

FOR THE

ASSEMBLY

Cardinal Joseph Bernardin
ARCHBISHOP OF CHICAGO

BASICS OF
MINISTRY SERIES

LITURGY
TRAINING
PUBLICATIONS

ACKNOWLEDGMENTS

Copyright © 1997, Archdiocese of Chicago: Liturgy Training
Publications, 1800 North Hermitage Avenue, Chicago IL
60622-1101; 1-800-933-1800; fax 1-800-933-7094; e-mail
orders@ltp.org. All rights reserved.

Editor: Gabe Huck
Production editor: Audrey Novak Riley
Designer: Anna Manhart
Production artist: Kari Nicholls

Cover photo: Antonio Pérez
Photos on pages 7, 24 and 27: Jennifer Brinkman;
page 15: Frank Casella; page 11: Eileen Crowley-Horak;
pages 3, 19 and 22: Antonio Pérez; opening page: John H. White.
This book is set in Goudy.
Printer: Thiessen Printers of Chicago

Bernardin, Joseph Louis, 1928 – 1996
    Guide for the assembly/Joseph Bernardin.
        p.   cm. — (Basics of ministry series)
    Includes bibliographical references.
    ISBN 1-56854-214-3
    1. Catholic Church — Liturgy.   I. Title.   II. Series.
    BX1970.B433 1997   97-8275
    264'.02'00977311— dc21   CIP

ISBN 978-1-56854-214-0
EGUIDE

CONTENTS

FOREWORD

Cardinal Joseph Bernardin left many things undone. In the 18 months between the diagnosis of cancer and his death in November of 1996, he began work on what he knew would be his last pastoral letter. He was writing about the liturgy as he had in his first letter as archbishop of Chicago just 11 years before.

Cardinal Bernardin knew that realizing the vision he set out in the 1984 letter would be a long task. In early 1995, in the *Decisions* document about archdiocesan priorities, he emphasized that all other tasks would be useless if liturgy and preaching were not given the highest priority and made excellent during the next years. Later that year, work began on a second pastoral letter on the liturgy. The plan was to publish this new letter in 1997 and at the same time make available a new edition of the 1984 letter, *Our Communion, Our Peace, Our Promise,* now to be called *Guide for the Assembly.* But the new letter was unfinished at Cardinal Bernardin's death. It seemed not only appropriate but important to go ahead with plans for this *Guide,* even if it must now stand alone.

For this new edition, Liturgy Training Publications has revised and updated the study tools found here. These were originally the work of Stephanie L. Certain. They are introduced on page 29.

The interests and the good work of Cardinal Bernardin ranged over many areas. But perhaps for him these were not many separate concerns. More than most of us in this bureaucratic time, he understood and lived toward integration. If here he speaks of liturgy's great importance, it is not in opposition to religious education, health care, schools, justice or the affirmation of life. It is rather that he believed that liturgy must take in and invigorate our whole world. Liturgy Training Publications offers Cardinal Bernardin's teaching on the sacred liturgy in gratitude for his life and his years as bishop of the church in Chicago, in gratitude for the blessing he was to us all.

—Gabe Huck

GUIDE FOR
THE ASSEMBLY

GREETINGS AND PEACE TO ALL OF YOU,

Catholics of this archdiocese, faithful and catechumens, for whom I   *1*
pray daily as your archbishop.

I have often written and spoken to you briefly about various   *2*
aspects of our work as a church and have asked for your support.
Now I want to write at greater length, not just about our work but
about our life. In speaking of the liturgy, I hope to reach and touch
the spirit of prayer in your hearts that spirit which brings us together
each Sunday for the eucharist. And I also have in mind those of
you whom infirmity prevents from joining physically in the celebration: Your prayer is part of every Mass we celebrate.

In December 1963, the Second Vatican Council completed   *3*
its first document, the *Constitution on the Sacred Liturgy*. Some of
you remember that time very clearly, but others have grown up in
the church since then. I want to speak to both: those who, like
myself, knew the forms of liturgy set 400 years ago and those who
cannot remember the Mass in Latin, the "last gospel," the altar
against the wall.

Most often when you and I meet, we celebrate the liturgy. As   *4*
we do, I realize more and more fully the truth of that great insight of
the bishops at Vatican II: "In the liturgy the whole public worship is

performed by the Mystical Body of Jesus Christ, that is, by the Head and his members" (*Constitution on the Sacred Liturgy*, #7). The liturgy is the action of God's assembled people.

5   In the past we often spoke as if the bishop or the priest alone celebrated the liturgy. But the evidence and the bishops' words at Vatican II are strong and definite: Whenever we gather as the church for Sunday Mass, for anointing the sick, for burying the dead — we celebrate the liturgy together. The *General Instruction on the Roman Missal* puts it simply: "The celebration of Mass is the action of Christ and the people of God" (#1).

6   We call this gathered church "assembly." It is you and it is I. Bishops, priests and deacons have unique roles in celebrating the liturgy, but they act as persons who serve the assembled people.

7   It is good theology and also good common sense, a matter learned not so much from documents and textbooks as from experience, that the assembled church celebrates the liturgy. I learned this saying family prayers in my home and at evening devotions in my parish church. I learned it also in these last decades which have been a time of renewal, making it more clear that the liturgy, while Christ's action first, of course, is also the action of God's people, who sing, listen to the scripture, praise and thank God, greet one another in peace, and share in the holy communion of Christ and the church.

8   This letter about the liturgy is sent to all of you, for you are the people who celebrate our liturgy; you are the assembly. In writing it I take for granted observance of all the church's liturgical norms, which provide a positive framework encouraging us to engage in creative, authentic celebration of the liturgy.

9   A few decades is very little time for so profound an experience to take hold, but at this point it is useful for us to ask ourselves how we are doing. I am going to ask you that, and ask it in a number of ways. I am going to chide a bit and challenge a lot. But I must say three things by way of introduction.

Introduction

First, thank you. I say that to all those who have labored to make the liturgy strong and beautiful: ushers, artists, musicians, writers, planners, lectors, cantors, deacons, servers, communion ministers, priests, sacristans — all who have accepted any ministry of service to the people of the parishes. Thanks especially to you who simply come to take your places and celebrate the Mass week after week.

The church in Chicago is known throughout the United States and even beyond for liturgical leadership which began long before Vatican II. In 1940 the first of those national gatherings that became known as "Liturgical Weeks" was held at our cathedral. Priests, religious and laity who studied and worked through these years helped prepare the way for the renewal that came from the

Council. Over the years, outstanding members of the Chicago church have shown by teaching and example what parish liturgy can be. I am thankful for all this work and zeal.

12   A second thing I must say simply to be certain we have a common foundation, a shared understanding of the liturgy. I understand the liturgy to be those rituals in which the church assembled expresses its very life. In our rituals we give thanks to God — for thanksgiving is the day-in, day-out attitude of the baptized; we intercede — for we are baptized to hold up all creation's needs to God; we read our sacred book, the Bible, and sing from our prayer-book, the psalms — for those words and prayers accompany us from childhood to old age.

13   From our parents and grandparents we have received the rites by which we give thanks, intercede, anoint and confirm, marry and bury. We do them over and over, and we teach our children to do them. Thus do we discover what it is to be a Christian and a Catholic. We learn this in hearing the word of God, in the hymns and acclamations, in the genuflections and the kneeling, in the greeting of peace, in sharing the consecrated bread and wine at the holy table. The liturgy is not an "extra," something nice that may give us good feelings. It is our life, our very spirit. It is the source of our identity and renewal as a church.

14   When we let the liturgy shape us — from the ashes of Lent and the waters of baptism to the broken bread and poured-out cup at every Sunday's Mass — then we shall find what it is "to put on Christ."

15   Yet liturgy is also a humble reality, and participation in liturgy does not exhaust our duties as Christians. We shall be judged for attending to justice and giving witness to the truth, for hungry people fed and prisoners visited. Liturgy itself does not do these things. Yet good liturgy makes us a people whose hearts are set on such deeds. Liturgy is our communion, our strength, our nourishment, our song, our peace, our reminder, our promise. This singular meeting with the Lord Jesus leads us to make all the events and circumstances of our lives occasions for meeting him. Liturgy is for me the bedrock of all my prayer and the measure of all my deeds.

My last introductory note is this: Over and over the Council stressed that the great goal for liturgical renewal is our "full, conscious and active participation in liturgical celebrations which is demanded by the very nature of the liturgy" (*Constitution on the Sacred Liturgy*, #14). Since those words were written we have only begun. The liturgical books have been revised so that the liturgy may indeed be celebrated in this way. But revising books and changing language does not make it happen. There is need for excellence on the part of all who minister at the liturgy, with all the artistry and hard work that entails. And yet even that is pointless until all who assemble to celebrate the liturgy have it in mind to participate together in this sacred deed.

The commitment I envision must be in our Catholic bones: the need to assemble each Sunday, to make common prayer in song, to hear the scriptures and reflect on them, to intercede for all the world, to gather at the holy table and give God thanks and praise over the bread and wine which are for us the body and blood of our Lord Jesus Christ, and finally to go from that room to our separate worlds — but now carrying the tune we have heard, murmuring the words we have made ours, nourished by the sacred banquet, ready in so many ways to make all God's creation and all the work of human hands into the kingdom we have glimpsed in the liturgy.

In 1978 the U.S. bishops reminded us that "God does not need liturgy, people do" (*Environment and Art in Catholic Worship*, #4). It is not an option, nor merely an obligation, not a bonus but a need — like food and drink, like sleep and work, like friends. "God does not need liturgy, people do." We need to gather, listen, give praise and thanks, share communion. Otherwise, we forget who we are and whose we are; we have neither the strength nor the joy to be Christ's body present in today's world.

It is true, of course — and indeed, this is a central truth about the Mass and sacraments — that the action performed is first and foremost Christ's. It is he who renews his act of perfect fidelity to the Father's will, he who welcomes new members into the community of the church, he who forgives and reconciles. In that sense, even liturgy "badly" celebrated is efficacious. Nevertheless,

16

17

18

19

the quality of *our* participation, of *our* action, is also important; that quality, in fact, enhances our participation in the action of Christ. Liturgy is not magic; we must bring to it the very best of which we are capable.

20   Although the liturgy expresses our whole life—our birth in baptism, our growth and forgiveness in reconciliation—here I shall speak only of the Sunday eucharist because it is our usual and regular way of gathering. How do you and I celebrate the liturgy each Sunday? If the liturgy is something done by the assembled people of the parish, how are we doing this task of ours?

21   I ask you to read what follows in a very practical spirit, thinking of your own parish and the Sunday eucharist there, and especially of your own participation in that Mass.

On Sunday, How Do We Gather?

Everything that happens before the first scripture reading is meant to help us assemble. That means gathering together many individuals as one community at prayer, but it also means recollecting ourselves personally — not by leaving behind the cares and distractions of home and work, but by bringing them into the gospel's light.

22

So we gather, one by one, household by household, passing through the doors of this parish church of ours, greeting one another, taking our places. This building called a "church" is a kind of living room of the family of God — it is *our* room when we assemble as the church. Here we are at home.

23

24   Its style differs from parish to parish. Its architecture and decoration may be in one tradition or another. What matters most is
that the room allows us all to gather closely, see one another's faces,
be truly present to one another. The common focus is the holy table
and near it the chair of the presider and the stand where the scriptures are read. But liturgy is not a performance, and we are no
audience. Liturgy is an activity, and the room itself should help
this happen. Many directives make it clear that in building new
churches and renovating old ones it is important to bear in mind
our need to see and hear one another, even as we see and hear the
priest, the reader, the cantor.

25   But even the best architecture can only invite us to come
together and pray together. That invitation must be accepted.
Certainly there are times for praying alone, seeking privacy, but the
Sunday liturgy is not one of these. The first task of each one who
comes on Sunday for liturgy is to take the open place nearest to the
holy table. Let our churches fill from the front to the back, and
if there are empty places, let them be the ones farthest from the
altar. The open places near the doors are then available for those
who may hesitate to draw closer because of some private need or
sense of alienation. Let them feel welcome whenever they come to
the church.

26   Every parish has members who care for the beauty of the
church building and the physical well-being of the assembly.
Sacristans keep this house for the church clean and beautiful.
Working with artists, they prepare the room for special feasts and
for the seasons. Ushers help people find places, and are truly servants of the assembly. They are models of the hospitality we should
all have as we greet one another.

27   One last note about these important moments before Mass.
As members of the assembly, we should be there — we should be
assembled — before the liturgy begins. Coming late or at the last
minute, if that can be avoided, says we are only spectators dropping

in to see a performance. But the liturgy is ours. To come late or leave early breaks the very spirit of the assembly. Come early instead, to greet others, to pray quietly, to center your thoughts on the Lord to whose table you have been invited. Come early and bring the concerns and problems that occupy you, all the people you carry in your heart.

How we begin the liturgy will vary somewhat from season to season and place to place. Always we make the sign of the cross, respond to the greeting of the one who presides, priest or bishop, and join in the opening prayer of the Mass. Usually we sing either an opening hymn or the "Lord, have mercy" or the Gloria. The familiar and lovely routine leads us into community prayer.

28

The sign of the cross should be made with reverence and attention. By this simple gesture we identify ourselves as Christians. This sign marked us even before baptism and will mark us even after death.

29

We respond to the presider's greeting and give him our full attention. When he extends the invitation, "Let us pray," we welcome the silent time to gather ourselves in stillness, so that we can enter fully into the opening prayer, unique to each Sunday, which places us in communion with the church throughout the world.

30

Singing within the entrance rite is a wonderful way for us to realize that we are a *community* at prayer. Cantors and those who play musical instruments select and gradually teach people those compositions which will draw forth their song. Here, and throughout the liturgy, music is not a decoration but part of the central action itself. What we do in liturgy is too vast and too deep to be left to our speaking voices. We need music so that we can fully express what we are about.

31

As the one who presides over the assembly, the priest has an important service to render in these introductory moments. Standing by his chair, he gives us his full attention as he leads us in the sign of the cross, greets us and invites us to join in the opening

32

prayer. Additional words, if any, should be very few, so that the cross, the greeting and the prayer stand out and are not rushed.

33   How the entrance rite gathers us and prepares us for word and eucharist will vary from one liturgical season to another. Art, music and words themselves tell us that we are again in Advent or Christmastime, in Lent or Eastertime, or in the Sundays of Ordinary Time. Commentaries and explanations should be superfluous.

34   If we gather as we ought — singing together, being silent together, responding together — we will be a community praying, and know that we are such.

How Do We Listen to the Word?

From the first reading through the prayers of intercession we are
engaged in the liturgy of the word. Most of our "doing" at this part
of the Mass is listening. On Sundays we listen to three readings
from the scriptures and the homily.

    This kind of listening is not passive — it is something *we do*.
At these moments in the Mass the liturgical action is not just
reading and preaching, it is *listening*. Readers and homilist are servants to the listening assembly.

    Often, though, we do not listen very well. Listening is a skill
that grows dull in the barrage of words one hears all day long. Yet
we have no substitute for it. In the liturgy we are schooled in the art

35

36

37

of listening. What we do here, we are to do with our lives—be good listeners to one another, to the Lord, to the world with all its needs.

38   We usually have a reading from the Hebrew Scriptures, one from the writings of the New Testament, and one from the Gospels. Every three years the church reads through most of the four gospels, much of the New Testament, and scattered selections from the Old Testament. The scripture selections themselves shape the liturgical seasons of Advent, Christmastime, Lent and Eastertime. During the rest of the year we generally read straight through the gospels and letters, picking up each week where we left off the week before.

39   The Council used the image of a pilgrimage in speaking of the church. We are on a journey, not only as individuals but as a church living out corporate life down through the centuries. On this journey we carry a book, our scriptures. Each week we gather, and in our midst the book is opened and read. Its words are heard over and over again. They have come down to us through dozens and even hundreds of generations. We in turn read them to another generation and so entrust the book to our children. In these stories, visions, poems, letters—all sorts of writing—we Christians find again and again the meaning of our own journey, the Lord who is our way and truth and life.

40   Our listening, then, is not like listening to a lecture, not like listening to a play. It is listening with the whole self, mind and heart and soul. We do not expect to be entertained or to learn new facts, but to hear God's word proclaimed simply and with power: the word of God spoken again to the *church*.

41   What helps us listen? Several things are important.

42   First: Lectors, deacons, and priests must read as the storytellers of the community. Entrusted with a sacred possession, our scriptures, they must live and pray with their scripture reading during the week before, practicing over and over, making it their own. They need to be capable of holding the attention of the assembly through their mastery of technical skills and also through their deep love for God's word and God's people.

It is a delight and an inspiration to me when I hear good lectors, women and men faithful to their task and trying to improve their skills. They truly struggle with God's word. Story and storyteller become one. Deacons and priests, as readers of the gospel, must work just as hard. The lives of all who read publicly should embody the words they proclaim. 43

The second element for good listening is this: Unless you have difficulty in hearing, I suggest that you give full attention to the reader and not rely on a booklet or hymnal containing the scripture texts. A reader lacks inducement to read as well as possible if others are following their own texts, for then the bond of communication is broken. We should fix our eyes on the reader and give full attention to the living word. 44

Third: It would be well if all of us who listen to the scriptures on Sunday prepared by reading scripture at home during the week — especially by studying and reflecting on the texts we will hear on the following Sunday. 45

Fourth and last: At the liturgy, the readings are to be surrounded with reverence, with honor. This means many things: reverent use of a beautiful lectionary, a period of silence after the first and second readings and after the homily, singing the psalm between the first two readings, a sung acclamation of the gospel. These are to be part of the normal pattern for Sunday Mass in our parishes. 46

The psalm is especially important. As we chant its refrain, we are learning the church's most basic prayerbook. The cantor is the minister who leads this sung prayer. While singing the psalm is perhaps not yet possible at all parish Masses, we can strive with all urgency to train parish cantors. The reintroduction of this ministry is one of the finest developments since the Council. The lectionary permits the use of the same psalm over a number of weeks so that people can become familiar with it. Gradually learning the psalm refrains by heart in the Sunday assembly, we can make them part of our morning or evening prayer each day. 47

48 We all recognize how important the homily is. You want good homilies; you need good homilies; you deserve good homilies. As parishioners, then, you must give your priests the time to prepare. Priests and deacons must both ask for that time, allowing others to take on various ministries in the parish, and then use the time well.

49 The homily is the assembly's conversation with the day's scripture readings. Only by respecting both scripture and the community can the homilist speak for and to the assembly, bringing it together in this time and place with this Sunday's scriptures. Good homilists must be familiar with the community's needs, pains and hopes. They must challenge and encourage. And they must seek out and listen to parishioners' comments. Those who preach should make frequent use of seminars and classes on homiletics and scripture.

50 Except for the most serious reason, the homily should not depart from the season and the scriptures. Homilies flow from the scriptures just heard, not from some other series of topics or themes. This is not a limitation on the content of homilies, for homilists who pay close attention to the cycle of readings will find ample opportunity to preach on the whole breadth of the gospel as it relates to contemporary life.

51 The reforms which followed Vatican II reintroduced the prayer of the faithful, the general intercessions, into the Roman liturgy. This prayer is a litany: One after another the needs of the world and the church are brought before the assembly, and to each we respond with prayer. When the intercessions are sung and the assembly responds to each with the singing of "Lord, hear our prayer" or "Lord, have mercy," it is clear that the intercessions are made by the people. Many of us remember how beautiful and strong a litany prayer can be when sung. The repetition of the chanted response reinforces the urgency of our appeal, and we realize our common priesthood in Jesus Christ, placing constantly before God all the troubles and needs of this earth.

How Do We Give Praise and Thanks?

Between the liturgy of the word and the liturgy of the eucharist we   52
have some rather quiet, practical moments. The collection is taken
and the gifts and table are prepared.

The collection itself is, according to the *General Instruction on*   53
the Roman Missal, "for the poor and the church" (#49). Bread and
wine are brought by the faithful, but so are gifts of money. This is a
true part of the liturgy. In this way we place what we have earned by
our work within the holy time of Mass. Unwilling ever to separate
our lives from our prayer, we bring something for the poor and the
church from our wealth or our poverty.

54   Now for the first time in the liturgy, our attention is focused
on the altar. We bring bread and wine to be placed there along
with the book of prayers. The unleavened bread is obviously not
our usual bread but a simple bread, a bread of the poor. In this
bread we cast our lot with the poor, knowing ourselves — however
materially affluent — to be poor people, needy, hungry. Unless we
acknowledge our hunger, we have no place at this table. How else
can God feed us? Ideally, because the bread is so important, enough
should be brought forward and consecrated each time for all the
people at that Mass.

55   We also bring forward wine. Like bread, it is "fruit of the earth
and work of human hands," something simple, something from our
tables, a drink of ordinary delight.

56   When the table has been prepared, we stand and are invited
to lift up our hearts to the Lord, to give thanks and praise. Thus
begins the eucharistic prayer in which we do indeed give thanks
to God our Creator for all the work of salvation, but especially for
the paschal mystery, that passover of Jesus whereby dying he
destroyed our death and rising he restored our life. The priest pro-
claims this prayer, but "the whole congregation joins Christ in
acknowledging the works of God and in offering the sacrifice"
(*General Instruction*, #54).

57   So this eucharistic prayer, too, is the work of the assembly.
That must be clear in the way we pray it. There is an immense challenge here. Centuries of practice shaped the assembly as spectators
rather than participants. We who are older grew up understanding
ourselves as lone individuals deriving what we could from prayer
and adoration while the sacred action took place at the altar. But
we are a holy people, called to praise God actively for God's saving
action in our lives.

58   In every eucharistic prayer the whole assembly joins the
proclamation of praise led by the priest. By singing the "Holy, holy,"
the memorial acclamation, and the "Amen," we claim the prayer
as our own. These acclamations are so important that even if we
sing nothing else at the Mass, we sing these affirmations of faith.

Every parish should have a number of melodies for them which everyone can sing by heart.

Nine texts for the eucharistic prayer have been approved in English. Priests and liturgy planners should be thoroughly familiar with them, so as to choose the prayer best suited to each season or Sunday.

These eucharistic prayers express in words the action we perform. All of us are becoming familiar with them. In the words of the old Roman Canon (now the first eucharistic prayer), Christ is present "for us," to bring us "every grace and blessing." In our newer prayers, "every grace and blessing" is spelled out in clearer detail. We thank God "for counting us worthy to stand in your presence and serve you," and ask that "all of us who share in the body and blood of Christ be brought together in unity by the Holy Spirit" (Eucharistic Prayer II); Christ is present upon the altar so that we may be filled with the Holy Spirit, "and become one body, one spirit in Christ" (Eucharistic Prayer III); we pray that we ourselves will become "a living sacrifice of praise" (Eucharistic Prayer IV). Renewed by the Holy Spirit, we lift up all the elements of life in praise and offer ourselves to be spent in sacrifice.

We are called to the Lord's table less for solace than for strength, not so much for comfort as for service. This prayer, then, is prayed not only over the bread and wine, so that they become Christ's body and blood for us to share; it is prayed over the entire assembly so that we may become the dying and risen Christ for the world. Participation in this great prayer of praise, as meal and sacrifice, transforms us. By grace, we more and more become what we pray.

The voice and manner of the priest should show that he offers this prayer as spokesman for everyone present. It is a *prayer* addressed to the Father. Not a homily or a drama or a talk given to the assembly, it embraces remembrance of God's saving deeds, invocation of the Holy Spirit, the narrative of the Last Supper, remembrance of the church universal and of the dead, and climaxes "through him, with him, in him."

59

60

61

62

63   For all our devotion to the body and blood of Christ present on our altars, we Catholics have hardly begun to make this eucharistic prayer the heart of the liturgy. It is still, to all appearances, a monologue by the priest, who stops several times to let the people sing. We seem as yet to have little sense for the flow, the movement, the beauty of the eucharistic prayer. How are we to make our own this prayer which is the summit and center of the church's whole life? How are we to see that this prayer is the model of Christian life and daily prayer? Does this prayer of thanks and praise gather up the way we pray by ourselves every day? When we assemble on Sunday, we help one another learn over and over again how to praise and thank God through and with and in Christ, in good and bad times, until Christ comes in glory.

64   Are we a thanks-giving people? Do we give God praise by morning and thanks by night? Do we pause over every table before eating, as we do over this altar table, to bless God and ourselves and our food? The habit of thanksgiving, of praise, of eucharist, must be acquired day by day, not just at Sunday Mass. In fact, it is at Mass that our habits of daily life come to full expression in Christ.

What Is Our Communion?

The communion rite begins with the Lord's Prayer and the peace   65
greeting, continues through the "Lamb of God" as the consecrated
bread is broken, moves into the communion procession, and con-
cludes with silent and spoken prayer. Here it is clear that the
assembly performs the liturgy; all of us pray the Lord's Prayer,
exchange the sign of peace, and join in the litany "Lamb of God,"
and all are invited to partake of communion.

    In their letter *The Challenge of Peace: God's Promise and Our*   66
Response, the bishops of the United States wrote, "We encourage
every Catholic to make the sign of peace at Mass an authentic sign
of our reconciliation with God and with one another. This sign of
peace is also a visible sign of our commitment to work for peace

as a Christian community. We approach the table of the Lord only after having dedicated ourselves as a Christian community to peace and reconciliation." So let it be in our parishes. When we greet those around us, let our words and manner speak of Christ's peace.

67   In the first decades of the church, the Sunday gathering was known simply as the "breaking of the bread." That gesture seemed to say everything. The loaf was divided and shared so that many might eat and become one. After our peace greeting has signified how we stand with those around us and with all the church, we attend to the priest as he lifts up the large host and breaks it.

68   Following the invitation to the table and the response ("Lord, I am not worthy . . ."), the communion procession begins. The communion of priest, deacon and communion ministers should never take so long that the communion of the people cannot follow directly on the invitation.

69   In most of our parishes now auxiliary ministers of communion assist the priest and deacon in taking communion to the people. This helps make it clear that we are *together* at this table, that this communion is the very image of the church and of that kingdom for which we live and die. Ushers contribute to the dignity and reverence of this sacred moment by helping the assembled community form a true procession and by offering assistance to those who may need it, such as the elderly, the infirm and the very young.

70   At this table we put aside every worldly separation based on culture, class, or other differences. Baptized, we no longer admit to distinctions based on age or sex or race or wealth. This communion is why all prejudice, all racism, all sexism, all deference to wealth and power must be banished from our parishes, our homes and our lives. This communion is why we will not call enemies those who are human beings like ourselves. This communion is why we will not commit the world's resources to an escalating arms race while the poor die. We cannot. Not when we have feasted here on the "body broken" and "blood poured out" for the life of the world.

Let that be clear in the reverent way we walk forward to take the holy bread and cup. Let it be clear in the way ministers of communion announce: "The body of Christ," "The blood of Christ." Let it be clear in our "Amen!" Let it be clear in the songs and psalms we sing and the way we sing them. Let it be clear in the holy silence that fills this church when all have partaken.

Before coming forward we say, "Lord, I am not worthy." We are never worthy of this table, for it is God's grace and gift. Yet we do come forward. This is food for the journey that we began at baptism. We may eat of it when we are tired, when we are discouraged, even when we have failed. But not when we have forgotten the church, forgotten the way we began at the font; not when we have abandoned our struggle against evil and remain unrepentant for having done so. Let us examine our lives honestly each time before approaching the eucharist. Worthy none of us ever is, but properly prepared each one of us must be. Christ, present in the eucharist and in us, calls us to be a holy communion, to grow in love and holiness for one another's sake.

When the priest is seated and the vessels have been quietly put aside, then stillness and peace are ours. Only after the meaning of the life we share has entered deeply into our souls does the presider rise to speak a final prayer.

What Does Our Dismissal Mean?

74   The concluding part of our Roman liturgy is very brief: the blessing and the sending forth. A procession through the assembly and a concluding song are usually part of this, but these are things the local parish needs to design for its own needs. Whatever is done in these final moments, including any announcements that have to be made, should help us pass from the moments of community ritual to less formal time together and then back to our own lives and daily prayers.

75   We are sent from the eucharistic table as a holy people always in mission. (The word "Mass" — in Latin *Missa* — means "sending" or "mission.") The spirit which fills us in the liturgy inspires us to re-create the world and in doing so to prepare ourselves for fulfillment in heaven.

In all we have done at Mass we have been uttering promises to one another, creating visions for one another, giving one another hope. Our hymns proclaim that faith is worth singing about. Our repentant prayers not only confess our own unworthiness but praise God's mercy and affirm our pledge to be merciful and seek reconciliation with all people. Our voices united in the acclamations express our willingness to be counted as witnesses to the gospel, with a mission to the world.

There is nothing narrow, selfish or blind in our Sunday worship. We give thanks not so much for personal favors from the Lord as for the earth itself, for the goodness of creation and the wonder of our senses, for the prophets and the saints and for our sisters and brothers throughout the earth, for God's saving deeds recorded in our scriptures and visible in our world. Only in such thanksgiving can we look on this world, embrace its sorrows and troubles, and confront the mystery of evil and suffering.

To give praise to God in such a world is to proclaim our own baptism into the death and the resurrection of Christ, a baptism that marks us for continuing conversion, the work of Christ's Spirit in us. We have seen and will continue to see sorrow and evil, yet we go on struggling, with songs of praise to God on our lips. This is, as Paul knew, nonsense to the world, but it is the way we have chosen. We are a people that lifts up songs of thanks over bread and wine which become for us the true presence of Christ. His coming was proclaimed in Mary's Magnificat, a coming marked by the removal of the mighty from their thrones and the lifting up of the lowly, by the hunger of the rich and the satisfaction of the hungry. Only those who live out that proclamation daily discover finally why it is not a dirge that we sing when we gather but praise.

The dismissal of the assembly is like the breaking of the bread. We have become "the bread of life" and "the cup of blessing" for the world. Now we are scattered, broken, poured out to be life for the world. What happens at home, at work, at meals? What do we make of our time, our words, our deeds, our resources of all kinds? That is what matters.

Our Progress in Liturgy

80   I cannot reflect on the eucharist without being aware of other concerns: how our celebration of Sunday Mass embodies our love for
young children, our solidarity with the handicapped, our response
to catechumens. I think, too, of that justice which we celebrate and
to which we commit ourselves at Mass. How can we— in liturgy
and in life —show the world a community where old age is loved
and respected, where the sufferings of the poor are known and
remedies are sought, where we can say with Paul that among us
"there does not exist male or female but all are one in Christ Jesus"?
I am conscious, too, of many matters of liturgical practice: among
them, the unnecessarily large number of Sunday Masses celebrated
in some parishes and how this adversely affects the quality of the

liturgy; my encouragement for communion under both kinds as prescribed by liturgical norms; my strong support for cultural diversity in the liturgies of Chicago's parishes — in language, music and other expressions where it truly manifests the Christian spirit of the people.

All of these things are important to me. I will look for opportunities to speak of them in the future. ₈₁

Whether you remember back before Vatican II or not, you know that these have not been easy years. We have had our problems in the liturgy. Where the Spirit of God breathes, there can be human excess, either of enthusiasm or reluctance. Liturgical renewal, like any other renewal, would be inauthentic without the mystery of the cross. Some have seen our liturgy as a mere means to teach or propagandize, some have trivialized it with unworthy songs and themes and needless comments and explanations, and some — perhaps saddest of all — have taken the renewed liturgy only as a set of directions, a kind of operating manual. One result of this last attitude has been to make the liturgy something mechanical and lifeless; the songs and words and gestures and the whole flow of the Mass fail to convey that this is indeed the action of the assembly. 82

Perhaps all that had to be. But now we need to ask: Are we ready for a deeper and more lasting approach to our Sunday Mass? Are we priests ready to work at presiding, to work at being members and leaders of the assembly? 83

Are we all, priests and parishioners, ready to say that the parish's commitment to liturgy may mean spending time and money? How else can we train good liturgical ministers? How else can we support staff people as coordinators of liturgy? How else can we pay just salaries to trained musicians who work with all aspects of liturgical music—with choirs, instrumentalists and organists, cantors and groups specializing in one or another style of music? How else can we build or renovate places of worship to make them truly "the house of the church," fitting places for us to assemble, listen, give thanks and share communion? 84

85   During these years, much of the liturgical renewal seems to have been concerned with external changes. The approach was practical. The revised books that have followed from the *Constitution on the Sacred Liturgy* have given us a marvelous form for our prayer. Now we need to make this liturgy ours, to be at home with it, to know it deeply, to let it shape our everyday lives. Further changes in rubrics and wording may indeed come, but our present task is to make beautiful and make our own the tradition we have received.

86   I encourage all of you, especially the clergy and all others involved in various ministries at the liturgy, to attend to the *Constitution on the Sacred Liturgy* in one very special way: Read it, read it again. When I go back to that initial work of Vatican II, I see what came from the liturgical movement, the courage of Pope John XXIII and the determination of the world's bishops — and the Holy Spirit working in all of them.

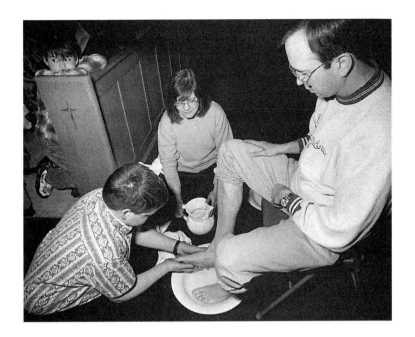

Conclusion

You know by now that I love the liturgy and find my own identity   87
there, as well as yours and that of the whole church. How glad I
would be to see all of us delighted and inspired by every Sunday
Mass in every parish! But good liturgy cannot be created out of a
bishop's letters or rules. I can only call you to be what Christ has
already called you to be. I can only invite you to serve God and one
another in the beauty and depth of Sunday Mass. I can only hold up
some goals and ideals, and pledge my own best efforts and the
support of the archdiocese. I can only keep you and the liturgy of
your parishes in my own prayer.

     Above all else, you must know, as I do, that we learn to pray   88
by praying. Can we take the treasure of prayer that is ours and begin

—alone or together—to pray as the church each morning and night? Can we keep Sunday holy? Can we take the Sunday scriptures and other passages of scripture into each week and even each day? Can we heed the bishops' call in our letter on peace—the call for prayer and fasting and abstinence on Fridays? Can we keep the great seasons of Advent and Christmas, Lent and Eastertime, not only in our churches but in our homes? Only in these ways will we gradually become active members of a Sunday assembly of the baptized who know how to gather, how to listen to the word, how to give thanks and praise, how to share in holy communion, how to take leave of one another for the week-long and life-long work of building the kingdom of kindness, justice and peace.

ARCHBISHOP OF CHICAGO

BRINGING THIS HOME
TO THE PARISH

INTRODUCTION

These are tools to help put Cardinal Bernardin's pastoral letter on the liturgy to work in the parishes. Everything here flows from the pastoral letter. Everything here depends on reading and reading again the words of Cardinal Bernardin.

The letter is addressed to all Catholics. Some of what follows speaks specifically to those on the parish staff or others involved in ministry at the liturgy, but the Cardinal's address to all should never be forgotten. The letter is not about some people doing good liturgy for other people. It is about the people doing their liturgy well. It is about ministers and priests who are first and last members of the Sunday assembly and so are determined to see that assembly exercise all its rights and all its duties in full, conscious and active participation. This participation in the liturgy is above all else why the church has set on this long and difficult course of renewal.

You will find three tools here. Any one of them may be useful beyond the main intentions of their creators.

For a Single Discussion
The first section can be used in a single session or a short series of discussions with any parish group. It presumes that

everyone has a copy of the *Guide* and is reading it. The discussion centers on discovering with Cardinal Bernardin the place of liturgy in parish life and the responsibilities all of us have to renew the liturgy through our participation. The tone of the meeting, like Cardinal Bernardin's tone, is to be one of enthusiasm and dedication to the needed renewal.

For a Discussion Series

The second section takes the seven names Cardinal Bernardin gives to the Sunday liturgy — our communion, our strength, our nourishment, our song, our peace, our reminder, our promise — and makes each one the starting point for a discussion. Each discussion then ranges all through the *Guide*. Such a series of discussions is especially appropriate for those who have taken on various responsibilities for the liturgy, but participation could well be open to any parishioners.

A parish might use both of these tools. For both, leaders should be prepared to work with small groups so that each person may be heard. These sessions are not meant to be lectures or presentations. Rather, the content of each session is meant to be found in the exchange of ideas and viewpoints among participants who have read the letter. Each discussion includes references to specific paragraphs in the *Guide*, references to appropriate texts in the *Constitution on the Sacred Liturgy* of Vatican II (the text can be found in *The Liturgy Documents* published by LTP), as well as some suggested readings from scripture. These readings could be part of evening or night prayer to begin or end the session.

For the Pastoral Staff and Liturgy Board

The third section takes the same approach as the Discussion Series but brings to it an awareness of the responsibilities of those engaged in decision-making and in preparing the liturgy. The questions and reflections here should be used with their corresponding topics in the Discussion Series.

Whereas the Discussion Series is meant to help all, staff and leaders included, come to and take part in the Sunday liturgy as responsible baptized Christians, this section pushes further. It says that the assembly has a right to full, conscious and active participation, and those who prepare the liturgy must establish practices that allow and encourage this. Cardinal Bernardin's letter is nothing if not practical, and this section moves toward parish application. These topics could be addressed over a period of months at staff or liturgy board meetings. At least one joint meeting of these two groups would enhance the likelihood of good communication among those who work together toward the renewal directed by the Cardinal's *Guide*.

As the parish liturgy is examined and careful plans are made to begin or continue its renewal, parts of the *Guide* as well as excerpts from the discussion questions may be reproduced in the parish bulletin or other materials to be given to parishioners.

Helpful Reading and Viewing

The annotated list of books, pamphlets and videos beginning on page 54 will be helpful in realizing the tasks and vision described by Cardinal Bernardin in his pastoral letter.

FOR A SINGLE DISCUSSION

"Liturgy is our communion, our strength, our nourishment, our song, our peace, our reminder, our promise. This singular meeting with the Lord Jesus leads us to make all the events and circumstances of our lives occasions for meeting him." (#15) All the baptized are invited to participate wholeheartedly in Sunday Mass. This has been true since the time of the apostles: On the Lord's Day, the baptized people assemble and celebrate the eucharist. This is not something we do for God but is God's good gift to us. To accept this gift is to give ourselves to the joyful and demanding participation described in the *Guide*.

Questions

1. Cardinal Bernardin says, "Liturgy is . . . the bedrock of all my prayer and the measure of all my deeds." (#15) Discuss what he might have meant by this. Does the Sunday liturgy influence your prayer and actions throughout the week? How?

2. "When we let the liturgy shape us—from the ashes of Lent and the waters of baptism to the broken bread and poured-out cup at every Sunday's Mass—then we shall find what it is 'to put on Christ.'" (#14) How do the actions of the Mass give a certain shape to Christian life? Consider the examples Cardinal Bernardin gives, but also discuss other objects, words, postures and gestures.

3. "Liturgy is not magic; we must bring to it the very best of which we are capable." (#19) What is that "best" for you? For your parish? What good habits would prepare you to participate more fully in the Sunday Mass?

4. "Are we ready for a deeper and more lasting approach to our Sunday Mass?" (# 83) What would this look like in your parish? Describe this in some detail.

5. Cardinal Bernardin asks dozens of questions in this letter. Select two or three of these that seem especially provocative to you and discuss them.

Resources

These paragraphs of the *Guide* should be especially helpful.

#4 – 7, Greetings

#13 – 14, 16 – 19, Introduction

#22, 24 – 25, 27 – 31, On Sunday, How Do We Gather?

#35 – 38, 40, How Do We Listen to the Word?

#63, How Do We Give Praise and Thanks?

#65 – 71, What Is Our Communion?

#82 – 83, Our Progress in Liturgy

#88, Conclusion

Additional help will be found in the *Constitution on the Sacred Liturgy*, articles 1, 10 – 12, 14, 48.

These scripture readings may be included in prayer and reflection at this gathering.

Psalm 118:24 – 29	Acts 4:32 – 35
Ezekiel 34:11 – 16	Ephesians 4:1– 6
Matthew 18:19 – 20	

FOR A DISCUSSION SERIES

Liturgy Is Our Communion

For most Catholics, "communion" has a specific meaning. We use it most often when speaking about the eucharist. We "receive communion" or "go to communion." Only rarely do we think about creating communion, participating in it, sharing it with others.

We enter into a relationship called "communion" when we share the body and blood of Christ at the Sunday eucharist. Here the entire liturgy—leading to and including the sacred meal—is an expression of our communion. Our Sunday liturgy, when the truth of our baptism in Christ is again affirmed, binds us together: rich and poor, servant and free, past generations and generations to come. We are a people, we are a holy communion.

Questions

1. Name the communities in your life — family, work, friends. How is the church community like these and not like these?

2. Do you regularly look toward Sunday liturgy as a time when you experience being part of a communion with Christ and with the people assembled? What contributes to and what hinders such a looking forward?

3. What moments at the Sunday liturgy build your sense of communion with people outside this local church? Why is this important?

4. In the scriptures, the word of God is spoken to a people. On Sunday it is proclaimed to the listening assembly. What is implied in this? How is this kind of listening different from ordinary ways you listen?

5. "This communion is why all prejudice, all racism, all sexism, all deference to wealth and power must be banished from our parishes, our homes, our lives." (#70) Do you agree? What are the main problems in doing this banishing? As a parish? As Catholics in this country?

6. "There are times for praying alone, seeking privacy. The Sunday liturgy is not such a time." (#25) What is your reaction to this? In the years since Vatican II, have we as church come closer to knowing ourselves as the body of Christ?

Resources

These paragraphs of the *Guide* should be especially helpful.

#24 – 31, On Sunday, How Do We Gather?

#37, 40, 44 – 45, How Do We Listen to the Word?

#57 – 58, How Do We Give Praise and Thanks?

#67 – 68, What Is Our Communion?

#74, What Does Our Dismissal Mean?

Additional help will be found in the *Constitution on the Sacred Liturgy*, articles 14, 19, 26, 30, 48.

These scripture readings may be included in prayer and reflection at this gathering.

Psalm 100	John 17:20 – 26
John 15:9 – 17	1 Corinthians 12:12 – 26

Liturgy Is Our Strength

Throughout the *Guide* Cardinal Bernardin refers to Christians as a people on a journey. We begin at the waters of baptism and we are never alone on the journey. We strengthen one another.

We find in the word and the table and in our assembly the courage to continue. And we "find again and again the meaning of our journey, the Lord who is our way and truth and life" (#39).

Without the liturgy, "we forget who we are and whose we are; we have neither the strength nor the joy to be Christ's body present in today's world" (#18). Liturgy is deep refreshment on our journey. We rest to remember the story of who we are, draw strength from brothers and sisters assembled, glimpse the reign of God and so resume the journey.

Questions

1. Day by day, what strengthens you? Think of exercise, art, conversation with friends.

2. Cardinal Bernardin says, "On this journey we carry a book, our scriptures." (#39) Do the scripture readings and the homily, the "assembly's conversation with the readings" (#49), challenge and encourage you? When this happens, is it personal or communal?

3. We share in the eucharist "when we are tired, when we are discouraged, even when we have failed" (#72). Is the Sunday liturgy a source of strength for people in your parish? In what ways? What more might be needed?

4. Have you ever thought that your presence at the liturgy is strength for others? How might your participation affect the lector, the cantor, the homilist, the person next to you?

5. Cardinal Bernardin thanks those "who have labored to make the liturgy strong and beautiful," and he includes many ministries (#10). Which of these ministries flourish in your parish? How does each ministry contribute to the Sunday liturgy?

6. Think carefully through the ways you prepare for Sunday Mass. What changes in your preparation would make you more ready to give full attention, full participation? Could the parish help this happen for more people?

Resources

These paragraphs of the *Guide* should be especially helpful.

#39 – 43, 46 – 49, 51, How Do We Listen to the Word?

#61, How Do We Give Praise and Thanks?

#72, What Is Our Communion?

#77 – 78, What Does Our Dismissal Mean?

Additional help will be found in the *Constitution on the Sacred Liturgy*, articles 24, 51 – 52, 59, 110.

These scripture readings may be included in prayer and reflection at this gathering.

Psalm 46	Matthew 11:25 – 30
Psalm 84:5 – 8	Matthew 14:22 – 33
Isaiah 35:1 – 4	Luke 24:30 – 35
Isaiah 40:28 – 31	

Liturgy Is Our Nourishment

We come to the liturgy hungry and thirsty for the word, for the assembly, for the body and blood of the Lord. We are nourished by the bread of life and by the community which shares in this banquet. We need the liturgy — "like food and drink, like sleep and work, like friends" (#18). We need to "gather at the holy table and give God thanks and praise over the bread and wine which are for us the body and blood of our Lord Jesus Christ, and finally to go from that room to our separate worlds . . . nourished by the sacred banquet, ready to make all God's creation and all the work of human hands into the kingdom we have glimpsed" (#17).

At the liturgy's table, we stand as equals. We are making an image of God's reign which we seek. At this table we accept the happy responsibility for feeding all the hungry and all the hungers of the world.

Questions

1. What are all the sources of nourishment in your life? Think about people, places, recreation, food.

2. The fast before communion used to begin at midnight. Today we are asked to fast for one hour before communion, a token, a reminder. This is a fast of anticipation and preparation. Can fasting make you aware of your need for the eucharist? What kinds of fasting might be needed in the hours before liturgy?

3. The collection is to be "for the poor and the church" (#53). For you, who are the poor? In what ways does your parish care for the poor? How often and by whom is that commitment examined? How important are working for justice and works of charity to the parish as a whole? Is there a growing sense of how this is bound to our Sunday eucharist?

4. Can you hunger for eucharist when your life is full? Can you hunger for eucharist when you can't buy next week's groceries?

5. Cardinal Bernardin speaks often of the beauty of the liturgy. Does this describe your parish liturgy? Consider the singing, the assembly's responses, the vestments and vessels. What else? Can you expect to agree on what is beautiful?

6. How is your daily prayer nourished by the Sunday liturgy?

Resources

These paragraphs of the *Guide* should be especially helpful.

#13 – 18, Introduction

#53 – 56, How Do We Give Praise and Thanks?

#69, What Is Our Communion?

#80, Our Progress in Liturgy

#88, Conclusion

Additional help will be found in the *Constitution on the Sacred Liturgy*, articles 33, 47.

These scripture readings may be included in prayer and reflection at this gathering.

Psalm 23	John 6:35 – 40
Mark 6:34 – 44	John 6:53 – 58
Luke 22:14 – 20	

Liturgy Is Our Song

Liturgy is our song. We sing the liturgy. Song is not a frill but is "part of the central action itself. What we do in the liturgy is too vast and too deep to be left to our speaking voices. We need music so that we can fully express what we are about." (#31)

Questions

1. On what occasions in your life do you join in festive song? What songs do you really like to sing? When is the singing at Sunday Mass as natural and full as those occasions? Do you take joy in singing at Sunday liturgy?

2. The psalms are our ancient and constant songbook. What psalm refrains and verses have you come to know by heart? (For example: "Taste and see the goodness of the Lord.")

3. Cardinal Bernardin regrets that "centuries of practice shaped the assembly as spectators rather than participants" at the eucharistic prayer (#57). Do you recognize what he means? At Sunday Mass does the eucharistic prayer—from "Lift up your hearts" until the great Amen before the Our Father—sound like a great prayer of praise and thanksgiving? Do you think it should?

4. "Are we a thanks-giving people? Do we give God praise by morning and thanks by night? Do we pause over every table, as we do over this altar table, to bless God and ourselves and our food?" (#64) Answer Cardinal Bernardin's questions, and then ask: How can you help each other in a habit of thanksgiving?

Resources

These paragraphs of the *Guide* should be especially helpful.

#12, Introduction

#31, On Sunday, How Do We Gather?

#46 – 48, How Do We Listen to the Word?

#56 – 58, 63 – 64, How Do We Give Praise and Thanks?

#71, What Is Our Communion?

#84, Our Progress in Liturgy

Additional help will be found in the *Constitution on the Sacred Liturgy*, articles 53, 83 – 84, 112 – 114, 118.

These scripture readings may be included in prayer and reflection at this gathering.

Psalm 95	Luke 10:21 – 22
Psalm 96	Luke 19:36 – 40
Matthew 6:9 – 14	Ephesians 3:14 – 20
Matthew 26:26 – 30	

Liturgy Is Our Peace

At liturgy "the meaning of the life we share can enter deeply into our souls" (#73). This is Christ's peace, not the peace the world gives. We never abandon the world when we enter the assembly. We bring its needs with us. We are that world. But we bring the world before the Lord.

Little by little, liturgy makes us peacemakers. It calls us to "let our words and manner speak of Christ's peace" (#66), to spread the good news of the Lord's peace to others. At liturgy, there is a peace — a communion — in spite of everything, not least our own selves. Liturgy asks that we "dedicate ourselves as a Christian community to peace and reconciliation" (#66).

Questions

1. Do you bring your cares with you to Mass as part of your prayer? Do you consciously try to bring the cares of the world? Does the gathering rite before the readings help you join yourself, cares and all, with this assembly?

2. Do the scriptures, homily and intercessions ever make you feel the tension between Christ's peace and the world's ways?

3. Do the prayers of the faithful, the general intercessions, in your parish call the church to true prayer for all the troubles and sorrows of the world? Do you find yourself carrying these concerns into your daily prayer?

4. When you give and receive the sign of peace, is it "an authentic sign of our reconciliation with God and with one another" (#66)? How can you make this sign more powerful?

5. "When the priest is seated and the vessels have been quietly put aside, then stillness and peace are ours." (#73) Does this describe your experience of the time after all have received holy communion? Are there other times at the liturgy that are deeply peaceful?

Resources

These paragraphs of the *Guide* should be especially helpful.

#22, On Sunday, How Do We Gather?

#66, 70, 73, What Is Our Communion?

#76, What Does Our Dismissal Mean?

Additional help will be found in the *Constitution on the Sacred Liturgy*, articles 6, 106. See also *The Church in the Modern World*, another document of Vatican II.

These scripture readings may be included in prayer and reflection at this gathering.

Psalm 122   John 20:19 – 23

Luke 6:27 – 38   Romans 5:1 – 8

John 14:27 – 31

Liturgy Is Our Reminder

Sunday liturgy reminds us of "what it is to be a Christian and a Catholic" (#13). The book of scriptures is read in our midst and the eucharistic prayer gives thanks for God's deeds. We pray for the dead and ask the intercession of the saints. We remember too those who are absent, those who are oppressed and those who suffer, and we remember those in power.

If we didn't gather at the Lord's table every Sunday, how long would we remember? We need liturgy, lest we forget.

Questions

1. When does life give you and yor friends and family a chance to recall the past, to enjoy memories?

2. At the liturgy, how are you reminded of what it means to be a Christian and a Catholic? Be specific about the words, gestures, objects, songs and postures.

3. Every family has a history — a story passed down from one generation to the next. Our liturgy of the word and the blessings of bread and of wine were part of Jewish prayer before the time of Jesus. In them he received his own story as a Jew. How does the liturgy tell us our story? Do we Catholics take hold and eagerly pass the story on to the next generation?

4. The unleavened bread at Mass may remind you that we "cast our lot with the poor" (#54). Does the tiny bite of bread and the

sip of wine ever remind you of those who are hungry? What implications does the Sunday liturgy have for issues of social justice and human rights?

5. The eucharistic prayer is filled with thanks flowing from the church's remembering. How much of that do you hear and take to heart? Can this be done better? How?

Resources

These paragraphs of the *Guide* should be especially helpful.

#39, 51, How Do We Listen to the Word?

#62, How Do We Give Praise and Thanks?

Additional help will be found in the *Constitution on the Sacred Liturgy*, articles 5 – 8, 47, 102.

These scripture readings may be included in prayer and reflection at this gathering.

Psalm 103

Mark 9:2 – 13

Luke 1:46 – 55

Liturgy Is Our Promise

When we participate actively, honestly and enthusiastically in liturgy, we make promises—to ourselves, to this gathered church, to God. "In all we have done at Mass, we have been uttering promises to one another, creating visions for one another, giving one another hope." (#76) We promise to live gospel lives, "to be a holy communion, to grow in love and holiness for one another's sake" (#72). We promise to "become the bread of life and cup of blessing for the world" (#79). All our promising is foolishness unless we have first believed a promise.

Cardinal Bernardin writes: "Participation in liturgy does not exhaust our duties as Christians. We shall be judged for attending to justice and giving witness to the truth, for hungry people fed and prisoners visited. . . . Liturgy makes us a people whose hearts are set on such deeds." (#15) We leave liturgy strengthened by the promise we have received, and with promises of our own to keep, "a holy people always in mission . . . to re-create the world and in doing so prepare ourselves for fulfillment in heaven" (#75).

Questions

1. How have you learned about promises, making them, keeping them?

2. What speaks to you of God's promises when you participate in the Sunday liturgy?

3. "Our voices united in the acclamations express our willingness to be counted as witnesses to the gospel, with a mission to the world." (#76) What do you find challenging in the words Cardinal Bernardin writes about the dismissal at Sunday liturgy (#74 – 79)?

4. Liturgy makes us "the bread of life and the cup of blessing for the world" (#79). How does this happen in your parish? How does it happen in the quiet work of ordinary Catholic people?

5. "How can we—in liturgy and in life—show the world a community where old age is loved and respected, where the sufferings of the poor are known and remedies are sought, where we can say with Paul that among us 'there does not exist male or female but all are one in Christ Jesus'?" (#80)

Resources

These paragraphs of the *Guide* should be especially helpful.

#15, 17, Introduction

#53, 60, How Do We Give Praise and Thanks?

#70 – 71, What Is Our Communion?

#79, What Does Our Dismissal Mean?

Additional help will be found in the *Constitution on the Sacred Liturgy*, articles 2, 9.

These scripture readings may be included in prayer and reflection at this gathering.

Psalm 105:1 – 15	Luke 10:1 – 11
Isaiah 49:8 – 15	John 6:44 – 51
Isaiah 58:6 – 10	Acts 1:1 – 9
Matthew 5:13 – 17	Acts 2:36 – 39

FOR THE PARISH STAFF
AND LITURGY BOARD

The reflection questions allow you to consider together the vision of liturgy in your parish. The evaluation questions encourage you to look at specific and practical elements of your liturgy in light of the *Guide*.

Refer to the parallel sections in the Discussion Series for other matters, for references to specific paragraphs in the *Guide* and further reading in the *Constitution on the Sacred Liturgy*.

Liturgy Is Our Communion

Reflections

1. Does our parish liturgy tend to turn inward, meeting the needs of the local community but failing to acknowledge how our catholicity binds us to other communities?

2. How do we make new people welcome? Is the responsibility widespread? Does our welcome extend to all those who are not in the mainstream of this particular parish? Who are they? How can our liturgical practice help?

3. Does this assembly participate on Sunday as if the liturgy was theirs to do? Is it?

Evaluation

1. Does our worship space have adequate facilities for the physically disabled? Are the ill and the aged in the community truly remembered?

2. Can the assembly see one another's faces (see #24)? (Cardinal Bernardin refers to *Environment and Art in Catholic Worship;* this document emphasizes the importance of such visibility.)

3. Where are the empty places in our church? Does this vary from one Mass to another? Does our church fill from front to back? How can we encourage people to take the seats "nearest to the holy table" (#25)?

4. Do we have too many Sunday Masses for the size of our building or the size of our community or the number of priests? How do we begin to deal with this? (See #80.)

5. Is our worship space in good repair and well cared for?

6. Are our ushers "models of hospitality" (#26)?

7. Do many people come to Mass late or leave early? Why? Are there practical things to do to minimize the distraction this causes?

8. What are we doing to help people be well prepared to hear the word on Sundays?

9. Does our communion rite speak of unity in the way the ministers come forward, in the flow of the rite from invitation ("This is the lamb of God . . .") to the procession of the assembly without delay? Is the procession hurried and impersonal or is it full of reverence? Does the singing begin immediately after the invitation and are the songs accessible to all? Is there sufficient quiet time for reflection after communion?

10. Do our dismissal rites "help us to pass from the moments of community ritual to less formal time together and then back to our own lives and daily prayer" (#74)? How? What provisions are made on a regular basis for that "less formal time" after Mass?

11. Do our ministers at liturgy see themselves first as members of the assembly and then as servants to that assembly? Do they exhibit a deep reverence?

Liturgy Is Our Strength

Reflections

1. "Faith grows when it is well expressed in celebration. Good celebrations foster and nourish faith. Poor celebrations may weaken and destroy it." (*Music in Catholic Worship, #6*) Consider various aspects of Sunday liturgy in light of this statement: for example, the music, the homilies, the pace of the celebration, the preparedness and competence of the ministers.

2. What is the bond between liturgy and catechetics in our parish? How can it be made stronger?

Evaluation

1. Does the parish provide well for initial training of people who serve in various ministries? Does it provide for in-service training at least once a year?

2. Is there merit in having "terms of office" for ministers?

3. Is excellence in presiding expected? In reading the gospel? What forums exist for critique and evaluation? If the parish occasionally has presiders who are not part of the parish, are they given adequate preparation so that the practices of this parish are respected at every Sunday liturgy?

4. Are the readings "surrounded with reverence and honor" (#46)? Do the lectors and gospel readers "hold the attention of the assembly through their mastery of technical skills and also through their deep love of God's word and God's people" (#42)? Do we use a beautiful book, one that encourages reverence for the word? Are the readings and the homily surrounded with time for silence and with strong singing of psalm and gospel acclamation (#46–47)?

5. Are our homilies the "assembly's conversation with the day's scripture readings" (#49)? Is there some opportunity for members

of the parish to participate in homily preparation and evaluation (as called for in *Fulfilled in Your Hearing*, the U.S. bishops' document on preaching)? Are homilists encouraged or required to take occasional workshops or seminars?

Liturgy Is Our Nourishment

Reflections

1. What do we hunger for? What hungers can the Sunday liturgy legitimately try to fill for parishioners?

2. What bonds are evident from our Sunday practices between those who celebrate this eucharist and the needs of the poor, those close by and those far away?

Evaluation

1. Does the bread we use give the full sign of being food? Is the bread made as a ministry within the parish?

2. Is enough bread "brought forward and consecrated each time for all the people at the Mass" (#54)? Why is this important? How can we achieve this easily?

3. Is the cup available to all at every Mass? Does the preaching occasionally invite reflection on taking the cup as well as on the whole mystery of the eucharist?

4. Are we nourished also by beauty in the liturgy? Consider the vessels used, the vestments and other objects. Do they evoke reverence? Do they meet the criteria (e.g., dignity and beauty in materials) set forth in *Environment and Art in Catholic Worship?*

5. Does the parish liturgy incorporate the arts of particular cultural groups within the parish? Can this be done in a way that neither patronizes the culture nor trivializes the liturgy?

6. Is the eucharistic prayer "the work of the assembly" (#57, see also #56) or is the assembly left to be spectators? Do we have a good "sense of the flow, the movement, the beauty of the eucharistic prayer" (#63, see also #61 – 62 and #64)? What steady practices will draw people into participation in this prayer?

7. Do the ministers of communion receive training when they begin and periodically get both practical and spiritual help? Do they serve with dignity and with reverence for the body and blood of the Lord and reverence also for the persons who stand before them?

8. Is our holy communion a procession or a line-up? Are all welcome at the table? Do we make it easy for children, the handicapped and the aged to share in the meal? Do ushers assist those who need help at communion? Does the preaching on occasion challenge the assembly with the notions explored in #70 – 72 of the *Guide*? Is the assembly aware of how this communion is shared with the sick and homebound through ministers of care?

Liturgy Is Our Song

Reflections

1. Is song natural and integral, or does it seem to be superficial or busywork for the assembly?

2. Are the psalms an important part of the community's prayer? What can be done so that people love the psalms and make use of them?

Evaluation

1. Does the assembly have a modest repertoire of excellent song worthy of being sung at liturgy? Do all expect to sing their acclamations, psalms and litanies (e.g., general intercessions, Lamb of God), as well as hymns?

2. Do the leaders of the ministry of music (cantors, choirs, instrumentalists, music directors) act from an understanding that the liturgy is to be sung by the assembly? Is the leadership mindful that most of our song should be known by heart?

3. Are we willing to pay trained musicians a just salary and provide for continuing education?

4. Are the presiders given help so that they can sing at least some elements of the eucharistic prayer, thus emphasizing the central importance of that prayer? Do presiders prepare all spoken texts, especially the orations? Do they make the sign of the cross and other gestures with reverence and attention?

Liturgy Is Our Peace

Reflections

1. In recent years, liturgy has sometimes been a bone of contention. If that has been true in this community, now turn to those areas where all agree on what is right, for example, the preparation of homilies or the reverent making of gestures. Are these the best they can be?

2. Sometimes "peace and justice" matters are assigned to a committee by that name. Does this community leave these entirely to the committee, or are these matters known to be the basic concerns of the gospel, needing the attention of all the baptized?

Evaluation

1. Do the general intercessions address the daily concerns of parishioners, and also matters that should be the concern of the whole church?

2. How is the sign of peace made at Sunday liturgy? Does the homilist ever probe the many dimensions of this gesture and its words?

3. Is there a deep sense of peace following holy communion?

4. What of the penitential rite? Is it rushed and thoughtless or, when used, an important part of entering into the word and eucharist? What ritual expression does it have in Lent?

5. How does the parish balance the needs of different language groups? What has been learned from successes in other parishes?

Liturgy Is Our Reminder

Reflections

1. Some parishioners naturally have more history and feel more rooted in the parish. Yet every parish always invites newcomers, both baptized and unbaptized, to find their home here. How does this evangelization lead to incorporation of the newcomers?

2. In what ways does the presence of an ordained presider— one who represents the bishop for this assembly—remind us that we are part of a larger church? Do the general intercessions do this also? What else?

3. How does the liturgy bring to our attention, week after week, that our mission is not to ourselves alone but to the world?

Evaluation

1. Marriages, baptisms, anointings, funerals: all these are the concern of the whole church, of all who come on Sunday. In what ways can the assembly's awareness of these parish sacraments be built up?

2. What efforts are made to bring the great seasons of the church into the homes of members of the assembly, with words, songs and rites that echo this Sunday's liturgy and also prepare us for next Sunday's liturgy?

Liturgy Is Our Promise

Reflections

1. How do we understand the promises made at baptism and renewed at Easter? What are we promising to whom?

2. What models do we have for the good celebration of Sunday liturgy? From which parishes can we learn? What is the ongoing promise of the staff and liturgy board to this parish church?

Evaluation

1. The dismissal rite is very brief. Is it as strong as possible? What is the "feel" of the space as people take leave of one another?

2. Does the sign of the cross or the taking of holy water serve as a reminder of the promises we have made and of what has been promised to us?

3. Is the collection seen as a true part of the liturgy, a promise being made and being partly fulfilled? Is it clear that the collection is always to be "for the poor and for the church" (#53)?

4. Is a commitment to mission clear in the way the assembly walks forward to holy communion, in the way the ministers share the body and blood of the Lord, in the songs we sing and the silence that follows (#70–72)? Does all of this speak far beyond words of who we are and whose we are (#18)?

HELPFUL READING AND VIEWING

These items are available from Liturgy Training Publications, 1800 North Hermitage Avenue, Chicago IL 60622-1101; 1-800-933-1800; fax 1-800-933-7094; e-mail orders@ltp.org.

Documents

The Liturgy Documents: A Parish Resource. This book contains the basic texts from Rome and from the U.S. Bishops' Committee on the Liturgy. These are: *Constitution on the Sacred Liturgy, General Instruction of the Roman Missal, Appendix to the General Instruction for the Dioceses of the United States, Lectionary for Mass: Introduction, General Norms for the Liturgical Year and Calendar, Directory for Masses with Children, Environment and Art in Catholic Worship, Music in Catholic Worship, Liturgical Music Today, Fulfilled in Your Hearing,* and *This Holy and Living Sacrifice.* Includes excerpts from *Ceremonial of Bishops.*

Los documentos litúrgicos: Un recurso pastoral. A Spanish-language version of *The Liturgy Documents.* Includes *Constitution on the Sacred Liturgy, General Instruction of the Roman Missal, Lectionary for Mass: Introduction, General Norms for the Liturgical Year and Calendar, Directory for Masses with Children, Environment and Art in Catholic Worship, Music in Catholic Worship, Liturgical Music Today,* and *La inculturacion de la liturgia en un ambiente hispano.*

Bishops' Committee on the Liturgy Newsletter: 1986-1990. Bishops' Committee on the Liturgy Newsletter: 1991-1995. These two volumes collect all the newsletters of the United States BCL. They document the Committee's decisions, interpretations, and introductions made in regard to liturgy in the United States.

Preaching from the Liturgy

Preaching about the Mass. Gabe Huck and others offer examples of homilies that unfold the Sunday liturgy and invite participation.

Saving Signs, Wondrous Words. David Philippart gives models for preaching about the basic elements of our rites.

The Mass

The Sunday Mass Video Series. The liturgy as it is celebrated at several outstanding parishes where leadership and parishioners have worked hard. These five videos can change attitudes and give excitement to the work.

> *The Roman Catholic Mass Today: Introduction and Overview.* The major rites and movements of the Mass are introduced with footage from four ethnically and regionally diverse parishes.

> *We Shall Go Up with Joy: The Entrance Rite.* Ministers and parishioners talk about their preparation for Sunday liturgy. See how this comes together at a parish in Albuquerque, New Mexico.

> *The Word of the Lord: The Liturgy of the Word.* At a parish in Las Vegas, Nevada, see the word of God proclaimed with respect and vigor. Those who read and those who preach talk about their ministry. Parishioners talk about what they need and hope for from the liturgy of the word.

> *Lift Up Your Hearts: The Eucharistic Prayer.* See a community in Cleveland, Ohio, prepare their table and enter into their prayer of thanksgiving and praise to God. Parishioners speak of the many ways their lives are energized at the table.

> *Say Amen! To What You Are: The Communion Rite.* The communion rite has flowered into song, procession and prayer that people long for at St. Henry's in Cleveland, Ohio. Parishioners tell how their lives lead to the table and how they go from it full of love and ready to serve.

The Communion Rite at Sunday Mass. Gabe Huck looks at all aspects of the communion rite and suggests ways to make it strong and beautiful in every parish.

The Eucharistic Prayer at Sunday Mass. Richard McCarron examines the life of the eucharistic prayer in a vision that reestablishes it at the heart of the liturgy.

From Age to Age: How Christians Have Celebrated the Eucharist. Edward Foley assembles a history of the Mass from the evolution of liturgical art, music, architecture, books and vessels.

The Basics

Liturgy with Style and Grace. A basic text for a liturgy board or any group wanting a series of readings and discussions on the liturgy.

A Common Sense for Parish Life. Not about liturgy as such, but about the way that liturgy and catechesis might relate. This is a workbook that should be used first by the parish staff.

Preparing for Liturgy: A Theology and Spirituality. Austin Fleming's classic for beginners, introducing them less to what to do and more to why to do it.

Ministries

We Gather in Christ: Our Identity as Assembly. This study book locates the liturgical ministries in a formational and inspirational discussion of the vocation of the worshiping assembly. Written by the Worship Office of the Archdiocese of Cincinnati.

A Well-Trained Tongue: Formation in the Ministry of Reader. Aelred Rosser's comprehensive and practical guide to being a lector.

Proclaiming the Word: Formation for Readers in the Liturgy. A training video that examines both the faith of the reader and the work of the reader.

Proclamadores de la palabra: Formación para los lectores en la liturgia. A training video for Spanish-speaking readers. Filmed originally in Spanish, not dubbed.

Handbook for Cantors. Diana Kodner writes to ensure that cantors are not only grounded in the techniques of singing but also in their leadership role in the assembly.

The Sacristy Manual. G. Thomas Ryan has left nothing untouched in this guide to the work of sacristans.

Serve God with Gladness: A Server's Manual. David Philippart takes seriously the ministry of acolyte as he delivers practical instruction about the server's responsibilities and catechesis about the different liturgies at which they serve.

How to Form a Catechumenate Team. Karen Hinman Powell discusses practical steps for selecting, forming and maintaining a strong team to support those seeking Christian initiation.

Seasons and Sacraments

New Life: A Parish Celebrates Infant Baptism. See in this video how a parish immerses infants during their Sunday liturgies.

This is the Night! A Parish Welcomes New Members. A video about one parish's scrutiny rite on the Fifth Sunday of Lent and baptism at the Easter Vigil. It is an amazing look at the power of our ritual.

Catechesis and Mystagogy: Infant Baptism. Pastoral ministers, catechists, liturgists and scholars discuss what it takes to minister to the parents and families who are bringing forward their children for baptism. This is an approach to ministry that goes far beyond "baptism prep classes."

Welcoming the New Catholic. Ron Lewinski helps every parish see initiation as more than a one-time sacramental celebration. It is a core ministry that engages the community all year long.

The Three Days: Parish Prayer in the Paschal Triduum. Gabe Huck's classic introduction to the heart of the liturgical year: the Triduum. The liturgies of Holy Thursday night, Good Friday and the Easter Vigil are examined in detail. Practical instruction abounds.

An Introduction to Lent and Eastertime. A 13-page booklet that can serve as background to discussion in any group.

Sourcebook for Sundays and Seasons. This annual publication remains one of the best resources for preparing the liturgy in accord with the sanctoral and seasonal calendars.

To Crown the Year: Decorating the Church through the Seasons. While it remains an essential resource for those responsible for the church's seasonal environment, Peter Mazar's presentation of the liturgical year is fundamental to the work of any parish's liturgy committee.